Contents

English

Maths

By Lynn Hannay

There is a whole world to be explored outside the classroom. Children spend quite a lot of time – I seem to remember from my teaching days and my own school days before that – just gazing through the window, longing to be out there. Of course, there is the natural longing to play outside, to run free, to have fun outdoors – and that is important, a vital part of growing up.

But, for teachers and children, that outdoor world can also be a great resource for learning – learning about nature and wildlife, about growing our food, about caring for our world, about taking responsibility for its conservation. And then there is also the kind of learning that supports work in the classroom. Here again the outdoors can stimulate interest and enthusiasm, whether for maths or literacy or art or music. It can teach children to observe, opening their eyes and hearts and minds to new ways of learning.

The best way I ever discovered of encouraging children to write – which was my particular enthusiasm as a teacher, of course – was to go out with them, all of us with notebooks, to sit and watch, to talk about it for a while and then to write and sketch what we saw, what we heard and smelt and felt. Then we would draw that world in words or in pictures. It opened worlds for them – and for me too, as a teacher and as a writer.

Michael Morpurgo

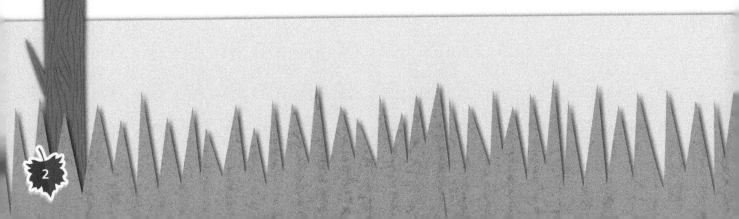

Introduction

This book is designed to help you take your teaching outdoors and into the school grounds. Each of the 30 activities focuses on specific maths and English learning outcomes, with National Curriculum links, and aims to inspire you to deliver lessons outside the confines of the classroom.

The practical tasks outlined in the book support a variety of learning needs and cater for all learners. The activities can also be differentiated according to the needs of your own class to ensure that each pupil can achieve the learning objective.

The book offers the following opportunities for differentiation:

Content of the activity – The content can be adapted to enable individuals and groups to engage in the activities with varying degrees of support. Similarly, the suggested reading materials can be adapted or replaced with easier or more complex texts.

Grouping – Working in groups or with a partner helps pupils to access knowledge, increase their understanding, develop concepts and practise skills; it also enables self-assessment, cooperation and mutual support.

Working in mixed-ability groups allows lower achievers to take advantage of peer support, whilst higher achievers have the opportunity to organise and voice their thoughts and to gain experience of explaining concepts and ideas. Roles can be allocated within the group according to each pupil's skill set and learning needs.

Working in ability groups allows for specific targeting of content and for a group of pupils working at a similar level to be allocated appropriate resources and levels of support.

Environment – It is important to consider the physical environment and demands of some of the activities, particularly if pupils have specific physical or medical needs, for example placing equipment for ease of access or considering visibility for pupils with visual problems.

Resources – Differentiating resources will allow pupils to access the activities at their own level. Some pupils may require adaptations to texts. Using a wide range of materials can allow a single learning outcome to be achieved by the whole class. A tablet device can enable a dyslexic or physically impaired pupil to achieve the desired outcome.

Pace – Each activity is designed to be completed in an hour. However, if some less able pupils find it difficult to complete tasks within the allotted timescale, the activity may need to be adapted. The extension activities can be used to challenge more able pupils.

Dialogue and support – Differentiation by dialogue can help to identify which pupils need detailed explanations in simple language and which pupils can engage in dialogue at a more sophisticated level. Questioning can be targeted to produce a range of responses, challenging more able pupils and enabling verbal support and encouragement to be given where needed.

Outcomes – The outcomes of pupil learning should demonstrate understanding of the knowledge or concept taught or mastery of the skill. Differentiation by outcome enables all pupils to undertake the same open-ended activity, but allows pupils to arrive at a personalised outcome according to their level of ability. This is useful, particularly for written work, and is embedded into many of the activities.

Assessment – By observing and questioning pupils throughout the activities, the lessons can be continuously adjusted according to the learners' needs. End-of-lesson assessments can be adapted according to the abilities of individual pupils.

Storytelling

National Curriculum links

Spoken language

- speak audibly and fluently with an increasing command of Standard English
- participate in discussions, presentations, performances, role play and improvisations
- gain, maintain and monitor the interest of the listener(s)
- select and use appropriate registers for effective communication

Vocabulary	oral traditions, intonation, tone, volume, audience
Resources	found objects from the school grounds; cushions, rugs or pieces of fabric; red, yellow and orange card; scissors; string; a pile of twigs and logs; a camera or tablet device
Prior learning	listening to and enjoying stories
Cross-curricular links	Drama – improvisation, role play; PSHE – self-esteem, working as a team, contributing ideas

Tell me a story

Activity

Allow the pupils to walk around the school grounds and find one object which they like or find interesting, preferably a natural object like a shrivelled leaf or an interesting-shaped twig or stone. Remind them to collect only things that are on the ground and not to pick any flowers.

Next, ask the pupils to form a circle on the grass by holding hands and sitting down. Now, in small groups, let the pupils choose a cushion, piece of fabric or rug to sit on and return to their place to sit down.

Tell the pupils they are going to build a 'fire' in the centre of the circle: use the pile of twigs and logs, cut the card into flame shapes, and fit them between the twigs and logs, using the string to secure it.

Settle down and explain to the pupils that long ago, before there were books and computers, people all over the world would gather together in a cosy, secure place around a campfire and tell stories. This is the oral tradition of storytelling.

The pupils are going to engage in creating a story together. They must listen carefully so that, when their turn comes, they can extend the story. They will take turns around the circle and add the next sentence – this prevents anyone from carrying on for too long. Ask them to keep their found object in their hand and to introduce it into the story at some point.

Start the process off, and join in and take a turn along with any teaching assistants.

Be aware of any pupil who feels they cannot contribute and offer support by asking questions.

Once you have been around the circle, recap the story so far and carry on. You may like to encourage actions and the use of intonation, and begin to allow contributions out of sequence if you feel this is appropriate.

 Extension activity: Back in the classroom, explain to the pupils that stories were told like this and passed down from generation to generation, changing and being embellished with each retelling, and that everyone remembers events and stories slightly differently. Invite the pupils to write down the story they just created and compare what each pupil remembered. Use these to create a wall display alongside a table display of the found objects. The pupils could recreate their 'fire' and storytelling circle in the corner of the classroom or library and be encouraged to use it themselves.

 Recording/evidencing: Take photographs or a video recording of the pupils taking part in the storytelling. This can be stored in the teacher's online storage system. Pupils can handwrite their version of the story for their books and / or a wall display, and you can add comments.

 Assessment methods: Observe the pupils' involvement in the activity and record significant observations. Consider your expectation of each pupil prior to the activity and evaluate against their performance at the end. Record your evaluation, making a note of each pupil's level of participation, listening ability and ability to communicate effectively.

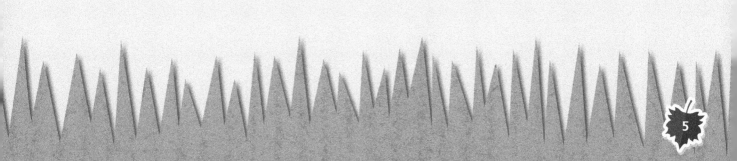

Composing non-fiction

National Curriculum links

Writing – composition

- plan, draft, write, evaluate and proofread
- discuss writing similar to that which they are planning to write in order to understand and learn from its structure, vocabulary and grammar

Reading – comprehension

- retrieve and record information from non-fiction

Vocabulary	facts, non-fiction, files, information, reference
Resources	a box of index cards with an alphabetical index and plenty of plain cards; pens, pencils, coloured crayons and marker pens; a selection of books on urban or rural wildlife depending on location, books about buildings, trees and plants, and identification charts and webs on plants, trees and insects; a camera or tablet device; a flip chart or free-standing whiteboard; an example of a fact file system, e.g. www.fishandkids.msc.org http://gowild.wwf.org.uk www.animalfactguide.com (These are all good examples to share with the pupils; some pages could be printed before the lesson for them to look at.)
Prior learning	some experience of retrieving information from non-fiction books
Cross-curricular links	Science – plants and animals, materials; PSHE – self-esteem, working as a team, contributing ideas; Art – sketching

Facts on file

Activity

Start your discussion with the difference between non-fiction/factual and fiction books. How do pupils recognise a non-fiction book?

Show the pupils some of the books and discuss what is important when writing in a factual way.

Show the pupils an example of a fact file and explain that this is an easy-to-use reference system in the form of cards. Explain that the cards usually have the same type of headings and information on them. Pupils may have examples of these at home.

Tell the pupils that they are going to make a fact file about the school grounds and ask them to come up with categories, such as flowering plants, grasses and non-flowering plants, trees, mini-beasts, building materials. Or just focus on plants.

Discuss what will go on each card (e.g. name, habitat, physical characteristics, nutrition, location in school grounds, a drawing, interesting facts/did you know?). The pupils will need to agree the headings for each category they will record. Write the headings on a flip chart so that the pupils can use it for reference.

Divide the class into groups and agree how to approach the investigation to avoid overlap and to ensure wide coverage. In larger school grounds the pupils will need to be supervised by teaching assistants. Make sure that the pupils understand that each group will be working together, but within the group every pupil should make at least one card, and all the cards must be about a different plant, animal, etc.

Tell the pupils that the books and identification charts are available for them to check facts and to find additional information but that they must use their observation skills and investigative powers first.

Visit the groups in turn to check progress and offer advice.

Bring the pupils together and allow time for proofreading before inviting them to share their fact files with each other. Allow time for the pupils to revisit their own cards and to make any changes or additions.

Discuss what they have learnt about the school environment and about creating fact files.

 Extension activity: Work together to file the cards and identify any obvious gaps. Consider if alphabetical filing is the best way or if filing under category works better. Could each card be filed alphabetically under each category? Ask the pupils to put forward ideas for where the fact file should be stored, how it can be used by other pupils and themselves, and how it can be added to.

 Recording/evidencing: The fact file will serve as recording/evidencing.

 Assessment methods: Observe the pupils and how they work during the activity. Record any significant observations and your evaluation. Look at the individual fact cards and assess how far each pupil has understood this genre.

Composing a story

National Curriculum links

Reading – word reading

• read aloud and understand the meaning of new words

Reading – comprehension

• use dictionaries to check the meaning of words

Writing – composition

• plan, draft, write, evaluate and edit their own story (write a shared story using words from the National Curriculum spelling list)

• read aloud their own writing, to a group or the whole class, using appropriate intonation and controlling the tone and volume so that the meaning is clear

Vocabulary	**Set 1** accident, accidentally, actual, actually, address, answer, appear, arrive, believe, bicycle, breath, breathe, build, busy/business; **Set 2** calendar, caught, centre, century, certain, circle, complete, consider, continue; **Set 3** decide, describe, different, difficult, disappear; **Set 4** early, earth, eight/eighth, enough, exercise, experience, experiment, extreme; **Set 5** famous, favourite, February, forward, forwards, fruit; **Set 6** grammar, group, guard, guide, heard, heart, height, history; **Set 7** imagine, important, increase, interest, island; **Set 8** knowledge, learn, length, library, material, medicine, mention, minute; **Set 9** natural, naughty, notice, occasion, occasionally, often, opposite, ordinary; **Set 10** particular, peculiar, perhaps, popular, position, possess, possession, possible, potatoes, pressure, probably, promise, purpose; **Set 11** quarter, question, recent, regular, reign, remember; **Set 12** sentence, separate, special, straight, strange, strength, suppose, surprise; **Set 13** therefore, though/although, thought, through; **Set 14** various, weight, woman/women
Resources	large flashcards with the Years 3 and 4 National Curriculum word list typed in large print (one word per card); plastic document holders and string; a notebook or lined paper and clipboard plus a dictionary per group; a list of where to find the cards for each group; a camera or tablet device
Prior learning	some knowledge of the word list and relevant spelling rules and meanings
Cross-curricular links	Computing – creating and publishing content; Art – decorate finished work and prepare for display and/or make a book; PSHE – cooperation, leadership, decision making, mutual support; Maths – tally charts

Trail a word

Activity

Before beginning the activity, place the flashcards in sets as indicated in the vocabulary table on the previous page around the school grounds. Put the flashcards in plastic document holders and secure with string to trees, fences, etc.

Tell pupils they will be following a word trail and will visit 14 stations. Divide the class into groups of four and ask each group to elect a leader who will ensure that everyone contributes and is listened to. Give each group a list of where the flashcards can be found.

At each station the pupils:

- read all the words aloud
- check that everyone understands what each word means (use the dictionary if needed)
- choose two words that will be used in writing a shared story
- write one or two sentences of their story together, underlining the chosen words for identification.

Note: Start each group at a different station to ensure there are no clashes.

Ask groups to return to you once they have completed the tasks at the first station so that you can check they are clear about what to do and have a good basis for their story. Once all groups have been checked, move around the stations to check pupils' progress and levels of cooperation.

After 15 minutes, bring all the pupils together to read their story so far to the class or another group. This helps to ensure that pupils stay on task and provides inspiration for those struggling for ideas.

Once the groups have completed the task, allow pupils to edit their stories for punctuation, spelling and interest and to prepare and read their completed stories to the class.

 Extension activity: Make a tally chart of how many times each word from the list was used and consider why some words were not chosen.

Pupils can write their stories in their best handwriting and prepare them for display in the classroom alongside the word list. The stories could be made into a class book with the word list at the back for reference. Individual pupils could create their own stories.

 Recording/evidencing: Stick copies of the pupils' stories in their English books. Take photographs of the activity to annotate and/or video the pupils as they discuss their understanding of the words, decide which words to include and write their stories.

 Assessment methods: Observe the pupils during the activity and mark the finished stories with the groups of pupils. Assess each pupil's knowledge and understanding of the words in the word list and their ability to use these words in their writing.

Personal writing

National Curriculum links

Writing – composition

- discuss writing similar to that which they are planning to write in order to understand and learn from its structure, vocabulary and grammar (write personal reflections, thoughts and feelings)
- draft, write, evaluate, edit and proofread a piece of personal writing

Vocabulary	personal, feelings, thoughts, ideas
Resources	notebooks or clipboard and lined paper and pens/pencils for each pupil; list of questions on a large chart which can be displayed progressively (i.e. only the questions about school grounds to start with)
Prior learning	experience of independent writing
Cross-curricular links	PSHE – improving facilities/environment, personal reflection, independence of thought and working

All about me!

Activity

Explain that today's writing is all about the pupils' thoughts, ideas and feelings. Tell the pupils that anything they write is personal to them so only you will be looking at it. Explain that no-one should ask anyone to share their work unless they wish to do so.

Ask the pupils to walk alone, in silence, around the school grounds, breathing deeply. Call them back after a few minutes. Encourage them to look around them and focus on the following questions: What do you like/dislike about the school grounds? Why?

Prompt the pupils by asking questions such as: Are there any areas you like better than other areas?

Now ask the pupils to spend five minutes writing down their answers.

Invite those who are willing to share what they have written; encourage discussion. This exercise should help pupils to begin to focus on their own thoughts.

Now widen the subject matter to enable the pupils to reflect and write in a personal manner.

Either continue with a series of questions for pupils to think about and allow them five minutes to record their ideas, or give them a choice of questions to write at length about, or choose one question for the whole class to write about, e.g.

- How do you feel (inside/emotions) today? Why?
- How does the weather make you feel today? Why?
- What makes you feel good/bad/sad/happy/unhappy/cheerful/excited when you are playing outside?
- What do you enjoy about being outside?

Discuss the type of vocabulary and sentence starters that are appropriate for personal writing (e.g. I feel that … When this happened it made me think about … If I was in that situation I might …).

Be aware of pupils who find this an uncomfortable process and who may need support.

Allow pupils time to edit and proofread their work before creating a final copy. Be sensitive to where the final copy is stored if pupils wish to keep their work private.

Bring the activity to an end by allowing time for pupils who wish to share their work with the class to do so.

 Extension activity: Pupils write about anything they wish, remembering that they are not writing a story or description but about their thoughts and feelings. Pupils put together a class opinion about the school grounds, considering their impact on it at present, and create a plan for possible improvements to present to the head teacher and governors. For schools with a school council, the ideas could be discussed at a council meeting.

 Recording/evidencing: Each pupil will record their personal writing in their notebook and transfer their final copy to their English book or onto paper.

 Assessment methods: Observe how pupils approach this work and record any significant observations. Mark the draft and final piece with the pupil and assess their ability to write from a personal perspective and record their thoughts and feelings.

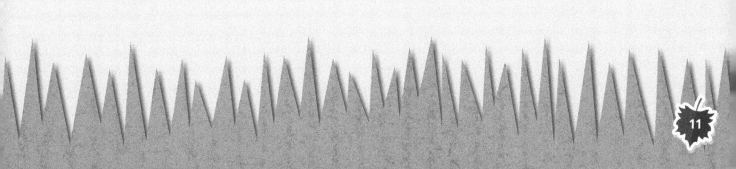

Writing a report

National Curriculum links

Writing – composition

- plan, draft, write, evaluate, edit and proofread (write a report)

Vocabulary	factual, objective, clear, concise, precise, report, bullet points, investigator, clues, speculation
Resources	chalk; red and white stripy tape; items for clues (e.g. moss, sticks and twigs, cardboard boxes, pebbles); clipboards, pencils, paper, paint, paintbrushes
Prior learning	some experience of the drafting process and writing in a factual way
Cross-curricular links	Science – working scientifically; Art – sketching and painting; PSHE – cooperation, decision-making, deduction, observation

I'm an investigator

Activity

Before the lesson, place a number of objects not too far apart in an area of the school grounds (e.g. a pile of twigs, stones and pebbles in a pattern; some moss or foliage; a cardboard box with holes in it; and a chalked paw print or two).

Before leaving the classroom, tell the pupils that the school caretaker has found some strange things in the playground and has asked if pupils from Years 3 and 4 could investigate.

Provide paper, pencils and clipboards to groups of four or pairs of pupils and explain that they must not touch anything, just use their eyes.

Once outside, ask the pupils to gather round and look at the scene. Let them spend a few minutes speculating about what they can see and how the objects got there.

Bring the talk to a conclusion and lead the discussion to the idea that an animal must have visited the school grounds and left them behind. Ask the pupils to make notes about the position, size and materials and to sketch them.

Move on to a discussion about what type of animal it might have been. Discuss each clue in turn and what it might tell you about the animal. Could it be a den? How big might the animal be? Could the animal have found the objects in the school grounds or brought them in?

Remind them that the school caretaker will want facts, not speculation.

Discuss how to write a factual report. Emphasise that it must meet several criteria – it should be factual, objective, clear, precise and concise and include the date and time. Explain that bullet points will work well for presenting the information.

Allow the pupils time to complete and label any sketches to add to their reports.

Invite one or two groups to read their reports to the class and comment on whether they meet the criteria – are they factual, objective, clear, precise and concise?

Give pupils time to edit their reports against the criteria.

 Extension activity: Now is the time for speculation – ask the pupils in their groups to write a story imagining what animal visited the school grounds. They could invent an imaginary animal and include details like a description, what it eats, its habitat, why it was there. Ask the pupils to draw or paint a picture of their animal and, using materials they can find in the school grounds, to build a den or nest for it. They can then draw or paint the den.

Create a class book of the stories and reports for the caretaker.

 Recording/evidencing: Publish the reports and stories in a class book or display. Stories and reports can be handwritten or photocopied to include in the pupils' English books.

 Assessment methods: Observe pupils as they work and note any significant progress and spontaneous use of knowledge and skills. Mark the reports alongside the pupil to clarify progress and assess their ability to write a factual report.

Instruction texts

National Curriculum links

Reading – comprehension

- identify how language, structure and presentation contribute to meaning
- learn the conventions of different types of writing, for example instructions (non-statutory)

Writing – composition

- discuss writing similar to that which they are planning to write in order to understand and learn from its structure, vocabulary and grammar

Vocabulary	instructions, poster, genre, appropriate, position, clarity, purpose
Resources	a selection of ready-made posters; A2 paper; markers, rulers, pencils, paint, paintbrushes and water pots; glue and glue spreaders; coloured and textured papers; a camera or tablet device; playground equipment (e.g. skipping ropes, balls)
Prior learning	different styles of writing for different purposes
Cross-curricular links	Art – graphics and illustration; PSHE – cooperation, taking turns, discussion and decision-making, giving clear instructions

Play that game!

Activity

Start by brainstorming with the pupils about the types of games they enjoy playing in the playground. Discuss what is important about these games and allow the pupils a short time to play. Try to focus on the types of games children create for themselves or traditional street/playground games like hopscotch, skipping, cat's cradle, tag and so on, rather than organised games like football. It can be as simple as collecting stones and pebbles to build with.

Ask the pupils to teach each other a game they may not know. The pupils can be divided into groups of different sizes for this activity.

Bring the class together and discuss what was important when teaching a game to a friend. Hopefully you will get clear step-by-step instructions and rules.

Now show the pupils a series of posters and allow them, in groups of four, to read and discuss one or two. Ask them what they notice about the posters. What are they for? What type and size of lettering do they have? Who are they aimed at? What makes a good poster? (e.g. clarity, size, illustrations that help get the message across or engage the reader, lettering you can read quickly at a distance)

Tell the pupils that they are going to create posters which will help other pupils to play their favourite playground games.

Show the pupils the A2 paper and discuss how to position their lettering and illustrations; explain that they must fill the sheet. Allow the pupils to choose paint, markers and coloured paper for collage, or to create sections on their poster, and to collect any natural objects like leaves to glue onto their poster to enhance it.

The pupils should work in groups of no more than four. Try to encourage them to present a range of games. Ask them to swap posters and see if they can follow another group's instructions.

Bring the class back together. Let the groups take turns to present their posters and receive positive feedback.

 Extension activity: The pupils can make A4 versions of their instructions and combine to create a book of playground games for the library; they could include a cover and a contents page. Alternatively, their small versions could be laminated for playground use. The posters could be framed in clear plastic and attached to the school fence or wall so that all pupils using the playground can read them and learn the games or, if this is not possible, they could be displayed inside the school.

 Recording/evidencing: The pupils' posters will serve as a record.

 Assessment methods: Observe each group during their work and record any significant observations. Assess each pupil's ability to understand what makes clear instructions; record notes or annotate photographs and store in the teacher's online storage system.

Adverbs and adverbials

National Curriculum links

Writing – grammar

- develop their understanding of the concepts set out in English Appendix 2 by using adverbs to express time and by using fronted adverbials

Vocabulary	adverbs, adverbials, time, verbs
Resources	chart stating: ADVERBS – can modify a verb (Usha soon started snoring **loudly**), an adjective (That match was **really** exciting!), another adverb (We don't get to play games **very** often) or a whole clause (**Fortunately**, it didn't rain); ADVERBIAL – a word or phrase used like an ADVERB to add detail or information to a verb. They explain HOW, WHEN or WHERE something happened (We met at her house **to play a game**); FRONTED ADVERBIALS start a sentence, so come in front of the verb (**On holiday**, he likes to swim); a sheet for each pupil titled 'Adverbs of time', divided into three columns with headings: When?, How long?, How often?; a sheet for each pupil titled 'Fronted adverbials', divided into three columns with headings When?, How?, Where?; a camera or tablet device for each group of pupils; pens/pencils and clipboards for each pupil
Prior learning	knowledge of sentence structure: nouns, verbs, adjectives, adverbs
Cross-curricular links	Computing – creating a video; PSHE – cooperation, team work, problem solving

Let's do it!

Activity

Note: This could be done as a whole-class activity while you take the photographs. Alternatively, the pupils could make a cartoon strip of drawings and sentences to record their favourite adverbs.

Distribute the 'Adverbs of time' sheets. Check pupils understand the function of adverbs and discuss the 'Adverbs' chart, explaining that adverbs can be divided into groups and can modify verbs, adjectives and other adverbs.

Brainstorm ideas to include in the columns on the 'Adverbs of time' sheet, for example:
- When: later, now, next, yesterday, next day, last year
- How long: all day, for hours
- How often: frequently, never, every day, sometimes.

Ask the pupils to work in groups of four to add to the list. Visit the groups in turn to ensure they understand the task and are adding appropriate adverbs to their list. Ask each group to say one word they added to each column.

Ask the pupils to use the playground, play equipment and sports area as a stimulus for writing sentences using some of the adverbs from their list (e.g. I like doing … for hours; Tomorrow my friend and I will play …; I never do … in the playground because …). Encourage pupils to take photographs to illustrate their sentences or to do a drawing.

Give the pupils time to put their photographs/drawings and sentences together before sharing with the class.

 Extension activity: Introduce the idea of fronted adverbials and ask pupils to complete the sheet by recording words in the appropriate columns, for example:

- When: suddenly, first, before lunch
- How often: every week, annually
- Where: at school, next to the shed, on the bus.

This activity can be concluded in the same way by writing sentences and then taking photographs to illustrate understanding of how to use fronted adverbials. For example: Every week, our school caretaker sweeps the school grounds. Before lunch, we line up in the playground.

 Recording/evidencing: The sentences and photographs will provide evidence and the pupils will have a record of words on the sheets which can be stuck into their English books.

 Assessment methods: Observe the pupils working and make a note of anything significant. Assess each pupil's knowledge of adverbs of time and fronted adverbials. View the sentences and photographs to further inform your assessment and mark the word lists for each pupil to check understanding.

Reading poetry

National Curriculum links

Reading – comprehension

- prepare a poem to read aloud and to perform, showing understanding through intonation, tone and volume and action (Years 3 and 4)

- listen to and discuss a wide range of poetry (Years 3 and 4)

- read and discuss an increasingly wide range of poetry (Years 5 and 6)

- learn a wider range of poetry by heart (Years 5 and 6)

- identify how language, structure and presentation contribute to meaning

Vocabulary	poetry, intonation, tone, volume, audience, rhythm, spring, personification, metaphor and other figures of speech
Resources	a copy of the poem 'Very Early Spring' by Katherine Mansfield for each pupil and/or one large copy for each group to view; a camera or tablet device
Prior learning	some experience of reading and discussing poetry and an understanding of figures of speech
Cross-curricular links	Science – plants (revise senses); Geography – the water cycle; Drama – performing; PSHE – self-esteem, working as a team, contributing ideas; Art – paint the scene in 'Very Early Spring'

It's spring!

Activity

Walk around the school grounds and ask pupils to look for signs of spring. Encourage them to use all their senses. Ask them to report back to the class what they see, hear, smell, taste (in the air) and touch. How does spring make them feel?

Read the poem 'Very Early Spring' to the pupils. Discuss:
- What is the poem about and what are the figures of speech used?
- What type of poem is it?
- What is the poet trying to tell the reader and how does she use language to do it?

Talk about the mood, atmosphere, rhythms, subject matter and how the poet engages the reader. How does the author feel about spring? What does she tell us about spring?

Read the poem again, this time in a monotone as if there is a full stop at the end of each line. Ask for pupils' reactions. Discuss how the author has used punctuation. Ask the class to discuss where they could use emphasis, intonation, tone, multiple voices and volume to make the reading more interesting. Read the poem again with the class joining in and using the suggested techniques.

Split the class into groups of four and ask pupils to elect a leader who will ensure that everyone gets to contribute. Ask the groups to prepare to perform the poem from memory to another class or in assembly.

Note: Some pupils will find it easier than others to memorise the poem and this may affect how you group the class.

Let each group perform and encourage positive critique.

Very Early Spring

The fields are snowbound no longer;

There are little blue lakes and flags of tenderest green.

The snow has been caught up into the sky—

So many white clouds—and the blue of the sky is cold.

Now the sun walks in the forest,

He touches the bows and stems with his golden fingers;

They shiver, and wake from slumber.

Over the barren branches he shakes his yellow curls.

Yet is the forest full of the sound of tears …

A wind dances over the fields.

Shrill and clear the sound of her waking laughter,

Yet the little blue lakes tremble

And the flags of tenderest green bend and quiver.

Katherine Mansfield

Alternatives: This activity could be repeated throughout the year.

For summer, try 'Midsummer Joys' by Winifred Sackville Stoner, Jr.

For autumn, try 'Fall, Leaves, Fall' by Emily Brontë.

For winter, try 'Snowflakes' by Henry Wadsworth Longfellow.

 Extension activity: Pupils revisit their performance after the critique to evaluate and improve upon it before performing for another audience. Read poems about spring by other authors and compare style and writing techniques. Pupils can write out the poem and sketch or paint images of spring to decorate their work.

 Recording/evidencing: The performances could be filmed and uploaded to the school's website or to video-sharing services (e.g. YouTube or Vimeo) or saved to the pupils' online storage/portfolio. Add comments to the pupils' handwritten poems.

 Assessment methods: Observe pupils' involvement in the activity and record anything significant. Evaluate each pupil's ability to read, understand and interpret the poem as well as their ability to commit to memory.

Composing poetry

National Curriculum links

<u>Writing – composition</u>

- plan their writing by identifying the audience for and purpose of the writing, selecting the appropriate form and using other similar writing as models for their own (write a poem about spring)

- plan, draft, write, evaluate, edit and proofread, selecting appropriate grammar and vocabulary

- perform their own compositions, using appropriate intonation, volume and movement so that meaning is clear

Note: This activity could be adapted for Years 3 and 4.

Vocabulary	poetry, intonation, tone, volume, audience, rhythm, spring, metaphor, simile, personification and other figures of speech
Resources	a copy of the poem 'Very Early Spring' by Katherine Mansfield for each pupil and/or one large copy per group which can be seen from a distance; clipboards with lined paper and a piece of A4 plain paper divided into six equal boxes (one per pair); pencils; information sheet about poetry styles for extension activity; flip chart and marker pens
Prior learning	experience of reading poetry and the activity 'It's spring!' (see page 18); an understanding and knowledge of figures of speech
Cross-curricular links	Science – plants (revise senses); Geography – the water cycle; Drama – performing; PSHE – self-esteem, working as a team, contributing ideas

It's spring: let's compose

Activity

Re-read the poem 'Very Early Spring' on page 19. Remind pupils of the structure, vocabulary, use of imagery, figures of speech, type of poem and what the author is trying to communicate to the reader. Tell them they are going to compose their own poems about spring.

Allow pupils time to re-acquaint themselves with signs of spring they can see. Encourage them to close their eyes, breathe deeply, listen carefully and ask them to consider how spring makes them feel. Encourage them to think about how the air feels on their skin, and what they can smell or taste in the air. Now ask them to look around and consider what they can see and touch.

In groups of four, ask the pupils to put a title in each of the six boxes: See, Hear, Feel (Emotions), Touch, Smell, Taste. Ask the pupils to write words in each box and to share their experiences with the group.

Bring the class back together and use the flip chart to brainstorm figures of speech and imagery related to spring. Ask the pupils to think of a metaphor for the clouds today and a simile for the sun, to use personification to describe the plants growing, etc. Encourage them to work in their groups and then report back to the whole class and create a bank of figures of speech and imagery. Discuss the effectiveness of the imagery.

Now ask the pupils to work in pairs to compose their own poem about spring using the imagery bank to help them. Tell them that the poem should have rhythm but should not rhyme, and it should have 13 lines.

Review pupils' drafts and then encourage the groups to work together to edit, proofread and evaluate until they are happy with the result.

Invite pupils to read their poems aloud and consider intonation, volume and movement. They can make more changes at this stage.

Alternatives: This activity could be repeated throughout the year.

For summer, try 'Midsummer Joys' by Winifred Sackville Stoner, Jr.

For autumn, try 'Fall, Leaves, Fall' by Emily Brontë.

For winter, try 'Snowflakes' by Henry Wadsworth Longfellow.

 Extension activity: Let each group perform their poem for the class and encourage positive critique. They can also perform for another class or in assembly. Pupils use the same subject/imagery bank to compose poems about spring in a different style.

 Recording/evidencing: The performances can be filmed and edited, then uploaded to the school's website or to video-sharing services (e.g. YouTube or Vimeo) or saved to the pupils' online storage/portfolio. Pupils can handwrite a copy for their books and you can add comments.

 Assessment methods: Observe the pupils and how they work during the activity, recording any significant observations. Mark the finished poems with the pupils and evaluate each pupil's confidence in planning, drafting and proofreading, as well as the creative content and structure of the poems.

Writing a story

National Curriculum links

Reading – word reading

- read aloud and understand the meaning of new words that they meet

Writing – transcription

- use dictionaries to check the spelling and meaning of words

Writing – composition

- plan, draft, write, evaluate, edit and proofread (write a story using chosen words)

- perform their own compositions, using appropriate intonation, volume and movement so that meaning is clear

Vocabulary	**Set 1** accommodate, accompany, according, achieve, aggressive, amateur, ancient, apparent, appreciate, attached; **Set 2** available, average, awkward, bargain, bruise, category, cemetery, committee, communicate, community; **Set 3** competition, conscience, conscious, controversy, convenience, correspond, critic, criticise, curiosity; **Set 4** definite, desperate, determined, develop, dictionary, disastrous; **Set 5** embarrass, environment, equip, equipped, equipment, especially, exaggerate, excellent, existence, explanation; **Set 6** familiar, foreign, forty, frequently, government, guarantee, harass, hindrance; **Set 7** identity, immediate, immediately, individual, interfere, interrupt, language, leisure, lightning; **Set 8** marvellous, mischievous, muscle, necessary, neighbour, nuisance, occupy, occur, opportunity; **Set 9** parliament, persuade, physical, prejudice, privilege, profession, programme, pronunciation, queue, recognise, recommend, relevant, restaurant, rhyme, rhythm; **Set 10** sacrifice, secretary, shoulder, signature, sincere, sincerely, soldier, stomach, sufficient, suggest, symbol, system, temperature, thorough, twelfth, variety, vegetable, vehicle, yacht
Resources	large flashcards with the Years 5 and 6 National Curriculum word list in large print; a dictionary with each set of cards; a notebook or lined paper and clipboard per pupil; a plan of the school grounds with locations of cards marked; a camera or tablet device
Prior learning	knowledge of the word list and relevant spelling rules and meanings
Cross-curricular links	PSHE – cooperation, leadership, decision-making, mutual support; Maths – tally charts

Find it!

Activity

Before beginning this activity, place the sets of cards and dictionaries around the school grounds. Tell pupils they will be working with a partner to follow a trail to create a story.

Give the pupils a plan of where each set of cards can be found. Tell them that they must visit each place marked on their plan. When they find each card they should take turns to:

- read all the words aloud
- check that they both understand what each word means (use the dictionary if needed)
- choose one word each from the list to create a shared story and both write them in their notes. They should choose words which they don't usually use in their writing.

Note: Tell the pupils they must not visit a station where another pair are working.

Allow the pupils about 20 minutes to complete the exercise. Move around the pairs to check progress, understanding and levels of cooperation. Bring all the pupils back together and discuss the word choices, checking for understanding. Ask the pairs to find a quiet spot and begin to note some ideas for an adventure story set in the school grounds. After five minutes, bring pupils back together to share ideas and gain feedback.

Pupils now use the words they collected to write their story, making sure all the words are included and underlining them for ease of identification.

Allow time for each pair to edit their stories for punctuation, spelling, interest and effectiveness and to prepare and read their completed stories to the class.

 Extension activity: Pupils handwrite their stories and word lists and prepare them for display in the classroom or for inclusion in a class book. Individual pupils could create their own stories using another selection of words. Make a tally chart of how many times each word from the list was used and consider why words were not chosen or proved popular.

 Recording/evidencing: Stick copies of the pupils' stories in their English books. Take photographs of the activity to annotate and/or video the pupils as they discuss their understanding of the words, decide which words to include and write their stories.

 Assessment methods: Observe the pupils during the activity and make a note of any significant observations. Mark the finished stories alongside the pairs of pupils to enable discussion for clarification and oral feedback. Assess and mark against your expectations of each pupil's knowledge and understanding of the words in the word list.

Signs

National Curriculum links

Reading – word reading

- read aloud and understand the meaning of new words that they meet

Reading – comprehension

- identify how language, structure and presentation contribute to meaning
- learn the conventions of different types of writing (create signs for the school grounds which are useful for different user groups) (non-statutory)

Writing – composition

- identify the audience for and purpose of the writing

Vocabulary	direction, sign, symbol
Resources	clipboards, paper, pencils and a range of different sizes and textures of papers and markers; a camera or tablet device
Prior learning	different styles of writing for different purposes
Cross-curricular links	Computing – using a tablet device for photography/recording and to create signs and graphics; Art – graphics and photography; PSHE – cooperation, taking turns, discussion and decision making

Show me the way!

Activity

Ask the pupils what they think is important about signs. What are they for? What type of lettering do they have? What makes a good sign? (Think about size, colour, fitness for purpose, clear information you can read quickly, positioning.) Talk about signs that indicate how to get around the school grounds and building.

Divide the pupils into groups of four and ask them to discuss the range of people coming to the school and what types of information would help them find their way around. Invite feedback. Hopefully pupils will have thought of: pupils; parents, grandparents and carers; visitors and tradespeople; teachers, governors, school staff; visitors with a disability and people for whom English is not their first language.

Ask the pupils, in their groups, to walk around the school grounds, remaining within the given parameters, and make a note of any signs they find relating to directions. They must take turns to read the sign aloud, then discuss any difficult words, the style of the sign and the clarity and relevance of the information it is giving.

Visit the groups to ensure pupils understand the task. Listen to their discussions. Set the pupils off at different starting places to avoid congestion.

Bring the class back together and go to the front of the building and grounds and consider the direction signs there.

Return to the school grounds and allow the groups time to discuss their findings and to consider if all groups coming to the school could find their way around.

Discuss how the signs in the school could be adapted to accommodate non-English-speaking visitors, younger school members or disabled visitors, especially those with poor sight, and any other groups identified by the pupils. (For example, entrance/garden/bike sheds – could these be in different languages? Braille? Are they at an appropriate height?)

Allocate each group the task of creating signage for a specified group of school users/visitors.

 Extension activity: Repeat the exercise inside the school. Use the information gathered to create a chart with small pictures of the signs down one side and the questions along the top (or ask the pupils to design their own chart). Ask the pupils to design a sign that they think is missing from the school grounds, using all the information they now have about good clear signage.

Ask the pupils to write to the governing body about how the signs around the school could be improved to support all school users.

 Recording/evidencing: Display the pupils' signs as a record of their work.

 Assessment methods: Observe each group during the activity and listen to each pupil reading a sign and each group discussing meaning. Record significant observations. Assess each pupil's understanding of what makes a clear sign and their ability to create appropriate signs for different groups of people.

Descriptive writing

National Curriculum links

Writing – composition

- plan, draft, write, evaluate, edit and proofread their writing (a description of the school grounds)

- select appropriate vocabulary, understanding how such choices can change and enhance meaning

Vocabulary	genre, description
Resources	notebooks or clipboards/lined paper and pencils/pens for each pupil; contrasting extracts of descriptive writing about place, e.g. *A High Wind in Jamaica* by Richard Hughes (Chapter 3: 'Exeter Rocks'), *The No. 1 Ladies' Detective Agency* by Alexander McCall Smith (Chapter 21: 'The House Behind the Trees'), *Hard Times* by Charles Dickens (Chapter 5: 'Coketown', starting 'It was a town of machinery …'), *My Family and Other Animals* by Gerald Durrell (Chapter 2: 'The Strawberry Pink Villa')
Prior learning	an understanding of the different genres of writing and their characteristics and functions
Cross-curricular links	Art – painting from a description, painting in the school grounds; PSHE – independent learning and working

Writing a picture

Activity

Settle the pupils in a quiet place and read one of the descriptive extracts to them. Ask them what type of writing it is and invite discussion about the use of language and how the author brings the scene to life.

Tell the pupils that the best descriptions 'write a picture' and that they should be able to close their eyes and see the scene. Ask them to close their eyes and read the extract to them again. Can they see it?

Read a contrasting piece and ask them to close their eyes as they listen. Again, discuss the use of language and the way in which the author brings the scene to life.

Tell the pupils they are going to 'write a picture' of the school building and grounds so that someone who has never visited can close their eyes and 'see it'. If the building and grounds are extensive, pupils can be split into groups and given one area to describe.

Ask pupils to walk around the grounds and make notes using a spider diagram with the words 'School' and 'Grounds' in the middle. Discuss what might be written on the spider arms (e.g. building, play area, garden) and remind them to use all their senses. Recap how to make useful notes without writing whole sentences.

Allow the pupils 10–15 minutes to gather their notes.

Read another descriptive extract to the class for inspiration and send them off to quiet places to begin to write their description. Visit the pupils in turn, offering support where needed.

After 10 minutes, stop the class and have them share their work with a partner and discuss together if the picture is coming to life and how they can improve their work.

Allow the pupils to continue to a completed first draft, then allow time for them to edit punctuation, spelling and flow.

Ask the pupils to find another partner to share and discuss their work with. Use the feedback to edit their work to improve vocabulary and imagery.

Ask for volunteers to read their work to the class.

 Extension activity: Write the finished description as a best copy or use appropriate technology to create a presentation version. Pupils re-read the extracts that were read at the start of the lesson and paint a picture from the information given. Discuss the results and consider if a stranger would be able to do the same with their descriptions of the school.

 Recording/evidencing: The notes, draft and finished descriptions should be kept and stuck into English books or displayed.

 Assessment methods: Observe the pupils as they work and note anything of significance. Mark the notes, drafts and finished pieces alongside the pupils, assessing their ability to choose specific vocabulary to enhance their description and their understanding of the purpose of descriptive writing.

Diary writing

National Curriculum links

Writing – composition

- plan, draft, write, evaluate, edit and proofread their writing (create an illustrated diary over the course of a week)

- use other similar writing as models for their own

- select appropriate vocabulary, understanding how such choices can change and enhance meaning (show an understanding of the type of language and style appropriate for a diary)

Vocabulary	diary, illustrations, personal
Resources	a new notebook or leaflet with alternate lined and plain paper and pens/pencils for each pupil; colouring pencils or watercolour paints; extracts from a range of non-fiction, fictionalised, historic and modern diaries (e.g. *The Diary of Anne Frank*, *Zlata's Diary: A Child's Life in Sarajevo* by Zlata Filipovic, *Diary of a Wimpy Kid* by Jeff Kinney, *The Diary of a Killer Cat* by Anne Fine, *The Country Diary of an Edwardian Lady* by Edith Holden)
Prior learning	knowledge of different genres of books
Cross-curricular links	Art – illustrating their books and designing and making a cover; PSHE – independent working, self-discipline, self-awareness

A week in the life of ...

Activity

Note: This activity is a week of activities (repeated each day).

Give each pupil a new notebook, preferably with both lined and plain pages.

Read aloud extracts from different types of diaries, including historical, modern-day and fictionalised diaries and illustrated ones. Discuss the style, use of language and personal nature of diary writing. On a flip chart, record the pupils' ideas and what they already know. Draw out the key features – chronology/sequence; first person; personal writing including thoughts, feelings and emotions; showing your own personality and style; usually written in the present tense in an informal style.

Brainstorm sentence starters that help with a sense of time (e.g. finally, before, later that day, eventually, afterwards).

Pupils write a week-long diary, which should focus on their observations of the comings and goings in the school grounds, how the playground is used, how the weather makes them feel each day and any changes they observe in particular areas of the school grounds and in the plants. They should include thoughts and feelings that are relevant to being in the outside environment. Include the option of a totally fictionalised diary where pupils can invent a persona through which to write; emphasise that the diaries can be private between the pupil and you if they wish. Encourage all the pupils to illustrate their diaries with sketches, watercolours, cartoons, etc.

Invite the pupils to find a quiet spot in the school grounds and to begin their diary writing, but also encourage them to move around to investigate different areas.

Visit each pupil in turn to discuss their ideas and offer support and advice.

Allow 5–10 minutes for pupils to edit and evaluate their work at the end of the session before handing in their book.

Collect the diaries and review the contents so that you can offer advice and support the next day.

Each day, allow time for a discussion about the process and for feedback from the pupils. Read a new extract from a diary for inspiration.

 Extension activity: Allow the pupils to take their diaries home over the weekend to add a further two entries that could be focused on their own garden or an outside space near to their home. Set a time for sharing extracts and reviewing the activity in class the following week. Pupils could design and make a book cover for their diary.

 Recording/evidencing: The diaries will be the evidence and record of the pupils' work.

 Assessment methods: Observe the pupils as they work and make a note of anything significant. Assess each pupil's understanding of the style and language appropriate to writing a diary.

National Curriculum links

Reading – comprehension

- pupils should be taught the technical and other terms needed for discussing what they hear and read, such as metaphor, simile, analogy, imagery, style and effect (understand, recognise and create their own imagery and figures of speech) (non-statutory)

Writing – composition

- select appropriate vocabulary, understanding how such choices can change and enhance meaning

Vocabulary	simile, metaphor, alliteration, onomatopoeia, hyperbole, personification
Resources	A1 sheets of paper per pupil divided into six sections; watercolour paints and brushes and marker pens; a camera or tablet device for recording; extracts from books using strong images
Prior learning	some knowledge of the range of figures of speech
Cross-curricular links	Art – watercolour painting

Close your eyes and imagine

Activity

Recap with the pupils that a figure of speech is a way of using words in a non-literal sense to help the reader bring an image to mind. Remind the pupils through questioning what the following figures of speech are:

- simile – always contains 'as' or 'like' to make a comparison
- metaphor – compares without 'as' or 'like' by saying one thing is another
- alliteration – repetition of the same letter or sound at the beginning of adjacent or closely connected words
- onomatopoeia – a word which sounds like what it is trying to describe
- hyperbole – exaggeration
- personification – making an object or animal sound as though it is a person.

Read aloud some examples of rich imagery. The following books may help:

It Figures! Fun Figures of Speech by Marvin Terban

The King Who Rained by Fred Gwynne

There's a Frog in My Throat! by Loreen Leedy

White Snow, Bright Snow by Alvin Tresselt

Gilberto and the Wind by Marie Hall Ets

Fireflies! by Julie Brinckloe

Give each pupil a piece of A1 paper divided into six sections. Ask them to write one of the figures of speech in each section of the table as a heading.

Challenge the pupils to create their own imagery/figures of speech – one for each section – inspired by the school grounds or the weather. Allow the pupils time to walk around and to sit quietly and discuss ideas with their friends before they decide on their imagery. Discuss the size of writing and presentation needed so that their imagery can be seen clearly when displayed.

Pupils clearly write their imagery/figures of speech in the appropriate section of their table, along with the type of figure of speech (e.g. simile) and then use the paints to illustrate them, taking inspiration from their surroundings.

 Extension activity: All the imagery and paintings can be compiled into a class book or wall display. Pupils can be challenged to create further imagery/figures of speech or to use their imagery in a piece of descriptive writing.

 Recording/evidencing: The paintings can be displayed and will stand as evidence, and can be photographed for inclusion in the pupils' online portfolios.

 Assessment methods: Observe pupils as they work and record anything of significance. Assess each pupil's confidence in their understanding and creation of imagery and figures of speech.

Discussing books

National Curriculum links

<u>Reading – comprehension</u>

- listen to and discuss a wide range of non-fiction and reference books (Years 3 and 4)
- read books that are structured in different ways and read for a range of purposes (Years 3, 4, 5 and 6)
- read and discuss an increasingly wide range of non-fiction and reference books (Years 5 and 6)
- recommend books that they have read to their peers, giving reasons for their choices (Years 5 and 6)

Vocabulary	non-fiction, reference, factual
Resources	a range of non-fiction books relevant to the school grounds, e.g. books about outdoor games and sport, plants and gardens, buildings, the seasons, the environment (include topics of specific relevance to your school and setting and ensure the books cover a range of reading abilities and, where relevant, include dual-language books); boxes for the books; paper, clipboard, pen or pencil per pupil; a plan for each pupil showing where they can find each selection of books and/or a large plan on a flip chart; a camera or tablet device
Prior learning	experience of reading, discussing and sharing books
Cross-curricular links	PSHE – cooperation, team work, making choices, self-discipline; other subjects depending on book choices

Join our book club!

Activity

Note: This activity works well with a large mixed-age group, so could be used to create a book club afternoon. Alternatively, it works well for guided reading. Place the book boxes in relevant areas of the school grounds (e.g. books about plants and animals in the school garden).

Tell the pupils that they are members of a non-fiction book club and are responsible for reviewing the school's books about the outdoor environment. Discuss with the pupils about caring for books and the particular care needed when using them outside.

Recap the words non-fiction, reference and factual, and check understanding.

Divide pupils into groups according to the number of book boxes. Allow the groups time to explore the books and to discuss their merits and purposes. Draw their attention to the cover copy/summaries and contents pages to help them quickly classify what they have.

Visit the groups in turn and ask key questions. (How might this book be useful? What type of information might you find in this book? Which books are not so useful? What makes you choose one book over another?)

Ask pupils to consider if their books provide sufficient information on the topic area. Invite pupils to choose the book they feel is of most use. The pupils should make a note of their choices – author, title, illustrator and publisher – and the reasons for their choice.

Bring all the pupils back together and ask each group, in turn, to talk about their selection of books, their choices and why they made those choices. Encourage the pupils to record any recommended books that interest them.

 Extension activity: Encourage pupils to record what is missing from their book box and to plan and organise a fundraising event to raise money for new books or write a letter to the head teacher with suggestions for improving the book collection. They could also research relevant book titles and work out costings.

 Recording/evidencing: Take photographs of the pupils working in groups and print one for inclusion in their English book. Ask them to explain the activity in writing. Video the groups discussing the books and the final presentations, and upload to the school's website or save to the teacher's online storage system.

 Assessment methods: Observe pupils during the activity and record significant observations, with a focus on attitudes to reading and ability to recommend books based on sound choices and reasons.

3-D shapes

National Curriculum links

<u>Geometry – properties of shapes</u>

- draw 2-D shapes; recognise 3-D shapes in different orientations and describe them (Year 3)

- recognise angles as a property of a shape (Year 3)

- identify right angles (Year 3)

- compare and classify geometric shapes, including quadrilaterals and triangles, based on their properties and sizes (Year 4)

- identify acute and obtuse angles (Year 4)

Vocabulary	cube, cuboid, cylinder, prism, triangular prism, cone, sphere, hemisphere, vertex, vertices, edge, face, right angles, acute angles, obtuse angles
Resources	images and models of 3-D shapes and their properties; clipboards; cameras or tablet devices; string and twigs; paper and pencils
Prior learning	2-D shapes and their properties; right angles, acute angles and obtuse angles
Cross-curricular links	Art – creating 3-D shapes; PSHE – cooperation, team work

3-D shape hunt

Activity

Introduce the pupils to a range of images and models of 3-D shapes. Discuss their properties using the correct vocabulary.

Give each group of four pupils a clipboard with a set of images of 3-D shapes and a properties/vocabulary checklist. Ask the pupils to explore the school grounds and identify natural or manmade objects which they recognise as being similar to the 3-D shapes on their sheet. Once they have identified several, provide a camera, tablet device or pencils and paper and ask them to photograph or draw their finds.

Back in class or outside, download the images and use a photo-editing program or app to label them with the name of the 3-D shape and its properties, or label their own drawings or printed photographs. Year 4 pupils should identify obtuse, acute and right angles in their shapes. Ask each group to share their work with the whole class. When all the images have been labelled, ask the pupils to classify the shapes by finding examples of different types of triangle (e.g. equilateral) and quadrilateral (e.g. parallelogram).

Ask the pupils to display their drawings and photographs and to play a guessing game ('e.g. I am thinking of a shape that has 12 edges, 6 sides and 8 vertices'). The rest of the class have to guess the shape and find drawings and photographs of it.

 Extension activity: Identify groups of 3-D shapes created as part of outdoor objects (e.g. cubes/cuboids within a climbing frame) or use string and twigs to make models of their 3-D shapes.

 Recording/evidencing: The pupils' photographs can be printed and added to their books, added to teacher records and/or displayed or published electronically. During the activity, observe the pupils and note down any significant comments/learning. Printed work or the pupils' drawings can be annotated with individual or group comments.

 Assessment methods: Observe pupils during the activity and question individuals and groups during the sharing back in class. Assess each pupil's knowledge and understanding of 3-D shapes and their ability to describe them using mathematical language.

Exploring lines

National Curriculum links

Geometry – properties of shapes
• identify pairs of perpendicular and parallel lines

Vocabulary	parallel, right angle, intersection, perpendicular
Resources	box of construction materials, e.g. cardboard boxes, natural objects found outdoors (pebbles, sticks, etc.) and/or building blocks; images showing parallel lines; cameras or tablet devices
Prior learning	right angles
Cross-curricular links	PE – movement; Art – patterns in nature

Lining up some learning

Activity

Show the pupils some images of parallel, perpendicular and intersecting lines. Tell them that parallel lines are unfriendly and never meet (but always stay the same distance apart), perpendicular lines are more friendly as they meet at a point and intersecting lines cross and continue, they are in a hurry so they are not very friendly!

Ask the pupils to demonstrate the different lines with their arms:
• arms straight up by their ears = parallel
• support the elbow of one arm with your other hand and hold the arm upright = perpendicular (point out the right angle created)
• cross arms in front of chest = intersection.

Play 'Simon Says' and call out the three types of lines and ask pupils to put their arms in the correct position. Split pupils into small groups to continue playing the game. The pupils should take it in turns to be the caller and you should visit each group to observe and check learning.

Ask the pupils to explore an area of the school grounds in groups of four and identify parallel lines; these could be on the ground, on the buildings, on natural objects or in patterns on their clothing. Once they have identified several, ask them to photograph their favourite three or record with pencil and paper.

Ask pupils to investigate whether all parallel lines are straight.

Give the pupils a box of construction materials, which could include items they find in the playground like sticks and pebbles and/or building blocks, and ask them to work in groups of four to create their own road system with parallel lines, perpendicular lines and intersections. Photograph their creations.

 Extension activity: Ask the pupils in groups to use their bodies to create examples of parallel lines, perpendicular lines and intersections. Take photographs of what they create.

 Recording/evidencing: Back in the classroom, print the photographs of the pupils' three sets of parallel lines, or use their drawings and create a class book of parallel lines around the school grounds. Ask the pupils to create a fact file about parallel lines to include in the book. Add photographs of the pupils using their bodies to create the lines if this extension is completed.

 Assessment methods: Observe and question pupils during the activity. Discuss the outcomes with each group of pupils for clarity. Assess each pupil's ability to identify parallel, perpendicular and intersecting lines.

Measuring length

National Curriculum links

Measurement

• measure, compare, add and subtract lengths (m/cm/mm)

Vocabulary	measuring, estimating, metres, centimetres, accuracy
Resources	five cones with a large letter attached to each (A–E); trundle wheel; long measuring tapes; metre sticks; clipboards, paper and pencils for each pupil; flip chart and markers
Prior learning	estimating activities in play situations; using various measuring tools; metres and centimetres
Cross-curricular links	PSHE – independent learning, decision-making, problem solving

Guess the distance!

Activity

Ask the pupils to set out the five cones in a random pattern on the ground, aiming for there to be a different distance between each cone. Identify for the pupils an area roughly the size of a tennis court or around 20 × 8 metres (a rectangular area helps to ensure that distances vary).

Ask the pupils to identify all the possible routes between the cones, and to systematically record them as a list (A–B, A–C, A–D, A–E, B–C, B–D, B–E, C–D, C–E, D–E). Give them a few minutes to do this and then discuss it as a class and create a chart of all possible routes.

Ask the pupils to walk between the cones and to estimate the distances in metres between each one. They should be encouraged to work individually and not discuss their estimations at this stage. Ask them to record their estimates. Bring the class together and discuss the estimations.

Demonstrate how to measure accurately using each piece of equipment.

Choose pupils to measure the distances to the nearest centimetre with the trundle wheel, and allow everyone to record the measurements. Then choose pupils to use the measuring tape and then the metre sticks to measure the distances and record the findings.

Ask the pupils to design a chart to compare their estimations and the results from using the trundle wheel, metre stick and tape.

Discuss the merits of each method of measuring and which they think was most accurate and why. Ask pupils to record their views underneath the chart they have made (e.g. provide time for pupils to compare their estimates with the actual results).

 Extension activity: Repeat the activity with the cones further apart. The greater the distance, the harder it is to estimate. Repeat using a greater number of cones and see how many more routes can be made. Use large squared paper to draw a diagram to scale. Pupils who are more confident could be encouraged to work to the nearest millimetre.

 Recording/evidencing: The pupils will record the results in their own chart.

 Assessment methods: Observe and discuss with the pupils during the activity and make a note of anything significant. Mark the charts with the pupils at the end of the activity and, while they are engaged in recording, discuss and clarify their understanding. Assess each pupil's ability to identify and measure using a range of equipment.

Bar charts

National Curriculum links

Statistics
- present data using bar charts (playground games)

Vocabulary	bar chart, tally, axis, column, row, data
Resources	pieces of 10 × 10 centimetre squared paper; A4 centimetre squared paper; box of equipment the pupils usually play with at playtime; clipboards, pencils and colouring pencils; rulers
Prior learning	know what a bar chart is and how to get information from one; be able to create a tally chart
Cross-curricular links	Art – drawing people in action; PSHE – working in a pair, working independently, making choices; Computing – create a bar chart using an appropriate app; Science – plants

What's your favourite ...?

Activity

Gather the pupils together near any fixed playground equipment they normally have access to. Allow them 10 minutes to play and to try out their favourite equipment and any they don't usually play with. Ask them to say what their favourite equipment is and why.

Give each pupil a piece of 10 × 10 centimetre squared paper and a clipboard and pencil. Ask them to draw themselves playing with their favourite piece of equipment. They should fill the paper with their picture, so that it can be seen clearly, and colour it in.

When the pupils have completed their pictures, bring them back together and ask them to use their pictures to create a block diagram on the grass or on a large sheet of card. Invite pupils one by one to add their picture to the chart. Make a label for each column along the bottom (e.g. ball, skipping rope, climbing frame) and for each row up the side (e.g. 1, 2, 3).

Ask the pupils to generate and answer questions about the chart (e.g. Which is the most/least popular piece of equipment? How many more pupils like skipping than bat and ball? What else can you learn from the block diagram?).

Give the pupils a piece of A4 centimetre squared paper. Ask them to draw a vertical line near to the side of the page and label this axis 'Number of pupils', then number the squares going up (reminding them that the numbers should overlap the lines, not fit the spaces). Ask them to draw a horizontal line near the bottom of the page and label this axis 'Types of activity', then label the squares across the bottom with the names of the activities.

Ask pupils to colour in a bar to represent the number of children who liked each activity. Explain that each square centimetre on their chart represents the 10 centimetre squared papers on which they drew their pictures. The pupils are now creating a bar chart. Note: This is not a scale, it is representation; but it is the start of teaching scale.

Back in the classroom, create a block diagram wall display using the pupils' pictures.

 Extension activity: Repeat this activity for plants found in the playground. Discuss categories first (e.g. types of trees, colours of plants). Collect information about the plants in pairs or split the class into groups and collect information about a designated category. Pupils should draw the plants or use a tally to collect numbers.

 Recording/evidencing: You will have a class block diagram as evidence and each pupil will have their own bar chart to stick into their maths book. The extension activity will provide the evidence for a pupil being competent at gathering data and creating their own bar chart.

 Assessment methods: Observe the pupils during the activity and record anything significant. Mark the pupils' bar charts with the pupils to enable you to assess their understanding.

Measuring perimeter

National Curriculum links

Measurement

- measure and calculate the perimeter of a rectilinear figure in centimetres and metres (measure a sports pitch)

- convert between different units of measure (and use their understanding of place value and decimal notation to record metric measures)

Vocabulary	perimeter
Resources	trundle wheels, long measuring tapes, metre sticks; clipboards, paper and pens for each group; a camera or tablet device
Prior learning	experience of using a range of measuring equipment and the need for accuracy when measuring; knowledge of place value to two decimal places
Cross-curricular links	PSHE – problem solving, cooperation, working as a team

Round the edge we go!

Activity

Tell the pupils that the lines on the school sports pitch (e.g. football pitch) will need repainting soon and it is important to know the length of the lines in order to work out how much paint will be needed. Explain that they are going to measure the perimeter of the pitch. The pitch you measure should ideally be rectilinear. Discuss the meaning of the word perimeter and how best they can calculate this and record the information they find.

Divide the pupils into groups and give each group a measuring tool (you may have two groups with trundle wheels and so on). Send the groups to different points on the pitch (or use more than one pitch if available) and ask them to measure the four sides, then add all four measurements together to find the perimeter.

Once the pupils have completed their measuring and calculations, bring the class together to compare results. Discuss the following points:

- what they have noticed about the measurements of the four sides (they should have noticed that the opposite sides are equal) and what this tells them about measuring perimeter
- the importance of accuracy and what to do about any discrepancies (hopefully most measurements will be in broad agreement and it will be obvious if any groups need to re-measure)
- the pros and cons of their equipment (allow groups to swap and re-measure if they wish)
- how results have been recorded (e.g. 6.3 metres or 6 metres and 30 centimetres). Pupils could be asked to record their answers in both ways.

Allow time for re-measuring, checking and recording.

Look again at the pitch. Can the pupils see different perimeters they could measure where the pitch is divided? Can they offer solutions to measuring the perimeter of a semicircle?

Allow pupils time to explore these options and to offer an overall measurement for all the lines which would need repainting.

 Extension activity: Ask the pupils to generalise a rule to calculate the perimeter of a rectilinear shape. Make a scale drawing using simple scaling (e.g. 1:10).

 Recording/evidencing: Pupils will record their findings in a group. This can be marked, photocopied and added to each pupil's maths book. Take photographs of the pupils engaged in the activity and store on the school network or in the teacher's online storage system and the pupils' online portfolios. The photographs could be annotated to indicate particular pupils and their progress in understanding perimeter.

 Assessment methods: Observe and discuss the pupils' methods and accuracy as they work and note anything of significance. Annotate the finished record with each group to clarify their thinking. Observe and question pupils during the activity. Note down pupils who have achieved, those who extended their learning and those who will need further activities to secure their learning.

Time graphs

National Curriculum links

Statistics

- interpret and present discrete and continuous data using time graphs

- understand and use a greater range of scales in their representations (non-statutory)

- relate the graphical representation of data to recording change over time (non-statutory)

Vocabulary	time graph, chart, scale, obstacles
Resources	stopwatches, clipboards, centimetre squared paper, pencils and rulers; metre sticks; equipment for an obstacle course (e.g. logs, PE bench, play tunnel)
Prior learning	experience of using simple scales and reading time graphs
Cross-curricular links	Computing – create a time graph using an appropriate app

Watch out for the obstacle!

Activity

Tell the pupils they are going to create a time graph showing how long they take to complete an obstacle course.

Ask the pupils what they already know about obstacle courses and discuss what they know about time graphs. Explain that they will create individual graphs showing their overall time and how long it takes them to reach specific points on the course.

Set the course so that pupils with timing devices are stationed at 5-metre intervals along a 25-metre course. They should record the time in seconds when a runner reaches them (e.g. at the 5-metre station they may record 8 seconds and at the 10-metre station they may record 16 seconds – they are recording the total length of time taken from the start of the course, not the time taken between obstacles). Set an obstacle such as a tunnel to crawl through at the 10-metre station and a second obstacle such as a pile of logs or PE bench to climb over at the 20-metre station. This will ensure there are periods of quicker and slower progress over the course.

Divide the pupils into groups of six and ask them to work together so that when one is completing the course the others are stationed along the course doing the timing.

Discuss the following:

- how to collect the data
- design of a chart on which to record the data
- how to use the timing devices to ensure accuracy
- how to organise to ensure everyone completes the course and takes a turn in timing others.

Once you have agreement, allow time for pupils to create their data collection chart and then complete the course.

When pupils have their data, discuss how a time graph might look and show examples. Discuss what their graph will show and how they can record it. Explain that periods of time in 5-second intervals should go across the bottom (horizontally) – the x axis. Make sure pupils label the lines, not the squares. Label this axis (e.g. 'Time in seconds – scale 5 seconds to 1 square'). Tell pupils that the distance should go up the side (vertically) – the y axis – at 5-metre intervals. Label this axis (e.g. 'Distance travelled in metres' – scale 1 metre to one square). The 5-metre intervals will represent the timing stations.

Note: Do not include the obstacles in the graph. These are only provided to add variation to the speeds recorded.

Allow time for pupils to complete their individual graphs, ensuring they understand to put a cross at the intersection of the time in seconds for each activity. They can join the crosses.

Encourage pupils to generate questions (e.g. Which part of the course did I complete most quickly? Most slowly? Why? Can I predict how long it would have taken me to run 25 metres without the obstacles?).

Encourage pupils to compare their graphs to the others in their groups. Who was quickest overall? Who was quickest at 5 metres? Was the person who ran fastest for 5 metres the fastest overall?

 Extension activity: In groups of four, using a different colour per person, instruct pupils to collate their data onto one graph. Use an app to create the time graph.

 Recording/evidencing: Pupils will create their own graphs as a record of the activity, which can be stuck into their maths books.

 Assessment methods: Observe the pupils during the activity and record anything significant, paying particular attention to accuracy when collecting data, understanding of how to create a complex graph and understanding of scale. Mark pupils' individual graphs against your learning objectives and the National Curriculum links.

Lines of symmetry

National Curriculum links

Geometry – properties of shapes

- identify lines of symmetry in 2-D shapes presented in different orientations
- complete a simple symmetric figure with respect to a specific line of symmetry

Vocabulary	symmetry, symmetrical, line of symmetry
Resources	clipboards, pencils, colouring pencils and trail sheets for each pupil; printed half images of symmetrical objects for pupils to complete
Prior learning	understand what symmetry is and identify a simple line of symmetry in a 2-D shape
Cross-curricular links	Art – creating symmetrical drawings and paintings

Symmetry trail

Activity

Prior to this activity, spend time taking photographs in the school grounds of symmetrical shapes. Try to include a range of types of objects (e.g. wheels, bricks, lettering, leaves). Divide them into shapes with one line of symmetry and those with multiple lines. Print the photographs and cut along one line of symmetry and use them to create a trail sheet for the pupils. The sheet needs to be organised in such a way that the pupils can find the object in the school grounds, complete the symmetrical drawing (make sure to leave space for this when printing) and identify if the object has one or more lines of symmetry. Include objects that are easy to spot, but also those in unusual orientations and positions to increase the challenge.

Ask the pupils if they remember what symmetry means. Most of the shapes will be 3-D, so they are looking for symmetrical 2-D faces, surfaces or outlines. Show them on a flip chart a picture of a simple symmetrical object and invite a pupil to draw on the line of symmetry. Next, show them a half picture which has a line of symmetry and one half of the object showing. Model how to complete the symmetrical drawing and explain to the pupils that they will be doing this in a symmetry trail.

Gather the pupils together and let them work alone or in pairs or small groups to complete the symmetry trail. Offer support where it is needed and observe the pupils as they work.

Once the pupils have completed the trail sheet, let them compare their drawings with your original photographs. Can the pupils find other symmetrical objects in the environment to draw and add to their sheet with the relevant information?

 Extension activity: Ask each pupil to fold a piece of paper in half and to draw a line down the crease, then to draw a shape on one half which uses the line as its centre. Swap with another pupil to complete the drawing and make it symmetrical.

 Recording/evidencing: Each pupil will have their completed trail sheet.

 Assessment methods: Observe and talk to the pupils as they work and make a note of anything specific and any pupils who appear to need additional reinforcement of these ideas. Assess each pupil's grasp of symmetry by marking their completed trail sheet and clarifying understanding through discussion.

Geometry

National Curriculum links

Geometry – properties of shapes

• compare and classify quadrilaterals and triangles, based on their properties

Vocabulary	quadrilateral, square, rectangle, rhombus, parallelogram, trapezium, kite, triangle, right-angled, isosceles, scalene, equilateral
Resources	large images of quadrilaterals with the name in large lettering on the back (square, rectangle, rhombus, parallelogram, trapezium, kite); large images of triangles with the name in large lettering on the back (right-angled, isosceles, scalene, equilateral [Note: Many right-angled triangles are also scalene or isosceles and pupils should have this drawn to their attention and be shown appropriate images]); A4 images of all the above with their properties on the back (two sets – for extension activity); 10 chairs; cameras or tablet devices; sticky tape; sticks, stones and string
Prior learning	understanding that 2-D shapes have properties which help to identify them; knowledge of the shapes in the game and their properties
Cross-curricular links	PSHE – confidence, independence

Let's play the shape game

Activity

Gather the pupils in the middle of a large open space in the playground. Place six chairs around the pupils in a circle at least 2–3 metres apart. Attach an image of a quadrilateral to each chair.

Call out the name of a quadrilateral and ask the pupils to run and stand behind the correct chair. Once all the pupils are confident with the names of the shapes, call out, 'I am thinking of a quadrilateral with four right angles and two sides of equal length.' Pupils should again run and stand behind the correct chair. Provide enough clues initially so that only one shape can be identified. Once pupils gain confidence, clues can be given which identify more than one shape, and they can be asked what other information is needed to identify a specific shape. Pupils should again run and stand behind the correct chair.

Once the pupils are confident with the properties, collect the images, mix them up and turn them over, so that you can attach the names of the shapes to the chairs. Repeat the game by calling out the properties.

Remove two chairs and repeat the game using the images of triangles, then the names of triangles.

Use 10 chairs and all the images of quadrilaterals and triangles and repeat the games. This should be done only when the pupils are feeling confident with their knowledge of quadrilaterals and triangles.

Pupils in groups of four could use sticks, twigs, stones and string to create their own triangles and quadrilaterals. Pupils can now draw or photograph the shapes they have made and use them to create a display.

Ask the pupils if they now feel more confident in their knowledge of these shapes and their properties.

 Extension activity: Divide the class into two groups – quadrilaterals and triangles – and let the pupils repeat the game by taking turns to act as caller, using the A4 sheets to help them identify relevant properties.

Pupils in groups of four can use their bodies to create quadrilaterals and triangles.

Pupils could make a bingo game with properties and pictures of the shapes to match up.

 Recording/evidencing: Take photographs of the pupils engaged in the activity and store on the school network or in the teacher's online storage system. The photographs you have taken could be annotated to show particular pupils and their progress in learning the properties of triangles and quadrilaterals. Give the pupils a sheet of quadrilaterals and triangles to name and stick into their maths books. This could be supplemented with a written quiz based on the game.

 Assessment methods: Observe the pupils during the activity and note anything of significance, especially any pupil who still seems unsure as the games progress and may need more support. Assess each pupil's knowledge and understanding based on the sheets they complete at the end of the activity.

Calculating area

National Curriculum links

Measurement

- calculate and compare the area of rectangles using square centimetres (cm^2) and square metres (m^2) (measure the area of a sports pitch)

Vocabulary	area
Resources	large sheets of centimetre squared paper cut to the size of a square metre; long measuring tapes, trundle wheels, metre sticks; centimetre squared paper; clipboards; large wooden protractors or right-angle measurers; masking tape, chalk
Prior learning	know how to calculate the area of a rectangle
Cross-curricular links	PSHE – cooperation, working as a team, problem solving

Area's the problem

Activity

It is often difficult for pupils to understand the concept of area, so you could begin by providing several metre squares of paper and asking the pupils to use them to cover a table, cutting some of them to fit. This provides a strong visual image of the square metre.

Reinforce this concept by giving pupils a large right-angle measurer and a metre stick and asking them to work in groups to mark out a metre square on the playground using masking tape or chalk.

Gather the pupils together on a marked-out sports court or pitch. Draw their attention to the fact that it is divided into geometrical shapes. Can they name them? How many of the smaller rectangles do they estimate would fit into the whole? How many different rectangles can they see?

Ask for ideas as to how they could measure the area. Can they estimate what the area would be? Show them a piece of centimetre squared paper cut to the size of a square metre to help them make their estimate.

Divide the class into groups and set them the task of measuring the area of the pitch. Have one group measure the whole pitch and the other groups take a rectangular section each. Discuss where the dividing lines are and whether they should measure inside or outside the lines. At the end, the smaller sections can be added together and compared to the results from the group measuring the whole pitch.

Ask each group to elect a leader who will ensure everyone's ideas are taken into account. Brainstorm how they will go about the task and ensure they understand how to generalise calculating the area of a rectilinear shape in terms of length × width. Emphasise the importance of accurate measuring. Ask the pupils to draw a freehand rectangle on paper, then to calculate the area of the pitch or their section of it and record their results on the rectangle.

Bring the class together and ask them to reflect on the activity and the challenges they faced.

Add together the results of the groups who calculated the area of the sections and compare the result to that of the group who measured the whole pitch. Discuss why there might be a discrepancy and perhaps re-measure if time permits.

Ask the pupils to compare the result with their initial estimate.

 Extension activity: Ask the pupils to make a scale drawing of their rectangle using a scale of 1 centimetre representing 1 metre.

 Recording/evidencing: Pupils will have recorded their measurements on their drawing and their calculations as a group. These can be photocopied and stuck into maths books. If you complete the extension activity, the scale drawings can also be photocopied and stuck into maths books.

 Assessment methods: Observe and talk to the pupils during the activity and note anything of significance. Mark the final record and calculation with the group and assess each pupil's understanding of how to calculate the area of a rectangular shape.

Line graphs

National Curriculum links

Statistics

- solve comparison, sum and difference problems using information presented in a line graph

Vocabulary	line graph, time graph, interval
Resources	clipboards, centimetre squared paper, coloured pencils for each group, stopwatch; snails, containers for the snails; metre rulers, tape measures; string, twigs, stones
Prior learning	being able to tell the time and accurately record time in minutes; creating and interpreting a range of graphs; difference, comparison
Cross-curricular links	Geography – field work, collect and analyse data, observation and recording; PSHE – problem solving, working as a team, cooperation, concentration

Snail journeys

Activity

Gather the pupils in the school garden where they will be able to collect snails.

Tell the pupils that they are going to collect data on how far a snail can travel over an agreed period of time and create a graph showing the time taken against the distance travelled. Discuss how to go about collecting the snails, how to treat them respectfully and handle them carefully, and any health and safety issues (e.g. washing hands and not putting fingers in mouths after handling snails). Pupils should remember where they collect the snails so that they can return them to their habitat after the activity is completed. Discuss how to collect the data they will need and how they might need to start again with a more active snail if needed.

How will they measure the tracks? How will they ensure accuracy in measuring?

Do they need to create a measurable space with an obstacle at each side to encourage the snail to move in a particular direction (e.g. a line of twigs or stones 10cm apart)?

How will they time the distance travelled?

What time intervals will be suitable – 5 minutes? 10 minutes?

Divide the pupils into groups of four and ask them to find a snail and collect the data. Observe the pupils as they are engaged in the activity, offering support as needed and acting as timekeeper.

Ask the pupils create a graph. Explain that the x axis (across) should be marked in units of time (e.g. 10 seconds per centimetre square) and should be labelled 'Time taken'. The y axis (going up) will show the distance travelled (e.g. 10cm per centimetre square) and should be labelled 'Distance'. Note: The scales will be dictated by how far the snails travel.

Ask the pupils to transfer their data onto the graph by putting an x at the appropriate intersection and then to join them together to create a continuous line. Ask the pupils to generate questions about their data (e.g. Can you predict how far your snail would travel in xx minutes? When was the snail quickest – at the beginning or at the end of its journey? Did it always travel at the same pace? Can they work out the average / mean speed (Year 6)?).

Ask the pupils to sit with another group and compare data. Whose snail travelled furthest? Whose snail travelled fastest?

Return the snails to their habitats as soon as possible.

Extension activity: Create a class graph on which each snail is shown in a different colour so that the data can be easily compared. This can be used to generate questions to enable the pupils to compare the data.

Recording/evidencing: Each group will have their own graph, which can be copied into their maths books.

Assessment methods: Observe and talk to the pupils as they are engaged in the activity and record anything of significance. Assess the final graphs and data collection by discussing them with each group in turn for clarity and understanding.

Exploring angles

National Curriculum links

<u>Geometry – properties of shapes</u>

- know angles are measured in degrees
- identify angles at a point and one whole turn (total 360°); angles at a point on a straight line and $\frac{1}{2}$ a turn (total 180°); other multiples of 90°
- use mental methods of calculation

Vocabulary	compass, protractor, angle, turn, north, south, east, west, north-east, north-west, south-east, south-west, clockwise, anti-clockwise
Resources	compasses; a large sign with '0' and 'N' on it; circular protractors; chalk; a camera or tablet device
Prior learning	how to use a compass
Cross-curricular links	Geography – compass points

Round and round we go!

Activity

Hand out compasses to groups of four pupils. Ask the groups to work out which direction is north. (Some teaching about how to use a compass may be needed.) Ask the pupils to identify south, east and west. Collect the compasses.

Ask the pupils to point north, jump to face south and then jump back to the north. Next, jump to the east and back to north. Finally, to the west and back to north. Get them to jump up and land facing either south, east or west, so that when they jump they show they know the direction they are going to land in. Always return to north. Do this lots of times until the pupils are secure in their responses, making it faster and faster. Introduce north-east, north-west, south-east and south-west and repeat the game. Alternatively, chalk marks on walls could be used and pupils could run to the north or west corners of the playground, etc.

Ask the pupils if they know what degrees are. Place a sign to the north so all the pupils can see it and ask them to face it. It should have a large '0' for 0 degrees and an 'N' for north beneath the 0. Ask the pupils to point to the zero and explain that they are facing north. Ask them to turn anti-clockwise to face west, still pointing, and tell them they have turned through 90 degrees. Ask them to turn back to face north and then turn to the south – they have turned 180 degrees. Back to north. Turn anti-clockwise and go around until they reach east (still pointing) – they have turned through 270 degrees. Back to north. Turn anti-clockwise and turn a full circle – 360 degrees. (Don't confuse them by turning clockwise yet.) Now repeat the activity, but calling out the degrees.

Ask the pupils to turn in either direction so that they begin to get the concept that 270 degrees one way around the circle is the same place as 90 degrees the other way. Call out 90 degrees clockwise or 270 degrees anti-clockwise. This is a very hard concept at first and needs lots of repetitive practice.

Finally, introduce the idea of 45 degrees in the same way using north-east, north-west, south-east and south-west.

Discuss with the pupils any tricks they know from skateboarding or BMX riding which are based around turns of various degrees. Challenge the pupils in groups to create a sequence of turns and jumps and runs using degrees and/or compass points as instructions. Can they write these down in a way that another group could follow?

Bring the pupils together and discuss what they have learnt.

 Extension activity: Introduce circular protractors and explore why the numbers go round in both directions. Have pupils stand at '0' while you call out a number of degrees. The pupils jump to this position. Ask the pupils to look at their protractors and point out that it says two different numbers. Ask them why this is. If one is 135, what is the other one? Ask the pupils how many degrees they must jump through to return to 0, going in the same direction. Repeat a number of times using different degrees.

 Recording/evidencing: Video the pupils taking part in the activity and store in the teacher's online storage system. Ask the pupils to record in their maths book what they have learnt – this will give you an insight into who has secure knowledge.

 Assessment methods: Observe the pupils as they take part and note any who appear to struggle with the concepts and need further practice. Do they understand that angles are measured in degrees and can they identify the turns in multiples of 90 degrees?

Creating a plan

National Curriculum links

Measurement

- solve problems (create a plan of the school grounds)
- use formulae for area

Geometry – properties of shapes

- draw 2-D shapes using given dimensions and angles

Vocabulary	scale, metre, centimetre, plan, right angle
Resources	large sheets of centimetre squared paper; marker pens; pencils; rulers, long tape measures, trundle wheels, metre sticks; large-scale set squares and protractors; a camera or tablet device
Prior learning	experience of measuring large areas, using scales, drawing right angles, reading and using plans; an understanding that a plan is an aerial (bird's-eye) view; it would be helpful if they had already created a small plan of the classroom.
Cross-curricular links	Geography – skills and field work (using maps and plans); PSHE – working as a team, solving problems

I've got a plan!

Activity

Take the pupils into the school grounds and tell them they are going to create a plan. You can:

- divide the class into groups and have each group create a plan of a different area, which are joined to form a plan of the whole school grounds (you will need to agree a scale, e.g. 1cm representing 1m is a good scale)
- have all groups create a plan of the same smaller area (one without too many difficult angles).

Show the pupils some plans and discuss the conventions of how certain features are shown (e.g. gates, fences, woodland areas) or have pupils create their own and put them into a key.

Brainstorm how to approach the task and the equipment they will need.

Split the class into groups and allow them time to elect a leader who will ensure all group members contribute. Allow time for them to discuss and plan a strategy, try out ideas and work out how to overcome any difficulties. Be ready to supply guidance and information as needed.

The group should sit together in the middle of their area and create a rough sketch before trying to measure it. This helps them to get an overall feel for the space. Pupils should use the rough sketch to write their measurements down, then translate this data into the scale drawing.

Let the pupils choose the equipment they will need, then give them as much time as possible to complete the task of measuring and recording onto their rough sketch and producing a finalised plan. Pupils must mark the measurements on their plan in decimal notation (e.g. 3.6 metres). Visit groups in turn to ensure they remain on task and are overcoming any challenges.

Bring the class back together to share the plans they have created and allow time for them to share how they overcame any challenges and anything they might do differently another time. If you have created a whole plan in parts, this is the time to lay it out altogether to see if it all joins up.

 Extension activity: Ask the pupils to work out the perimeter of the planned area, and to calculate its area by dividing their plan into recognisable geometric shapes.

 Recording/evidencing: The pupils will have their group plans as a record. Photograph each group with their plan and print a copy for each pupil's maths book and add to the teacher's online storage system. They can write a few sentences to record what they did, how they did it and what the challenges were.

 Assessment methods: Observe and discuss the activity with the groups as they work and record anything of significance. Talk to each group about their plan and assess each pupil's ability to create a large-scale plan, accuracy in measuring and understanding of scale.

Exploring the mean

National Curriculum links

Statistics

- calculate and interpret the mean as an average

- solve a wide range of problems including increasingly complex arithmetic

Vocabulary	mean
Resources	equipment to mark out a long jump area; clipboards, squared paper and pencils for each pupil; measuring equipment (e.g. metre sticks); calculators; a camera or tablet device
Prior learning	how to work out the mean
Cross-curricular links	PE – athletics; PSHE – problem solving, working as a team, tolerance

Don't be mean!

Activity

Tell the pupils they will be practising the long jump. They will be competing against themselves and each pupil must complete five jumps. Divide the class into four groups.

Gather the pupils on the grass and mark out an area for each group with a suitable run-up and a take-off point. Decide the rules (e.g. is the landing measured from where the feet land or is a bottom on the ground acceptable?).

Each pupil must design a chart on which to record their jumps in metres and centimetres and in metres only (e.g. 1.4 metres). Pupils take turns to measure, jump and act as linesperson or decision maker. Ask pupils to complete five jumps each and to record their distances.

Once all the pupils have collected their data, gather them together and ask them to use their data to work out their mean jumping distance.

Ask the pupils to work in their groups to collate their data into one table. This will involve some discussion, problem solving and cooperation. Can they use their table to calculate the mean for the whole group?

Ask them to generate some questions about their data (e.g. Who had the longest jump? Does the person with the longest jump also have the longest mean jump?).

Bring the class together and discuss what they can learn from the data they collected and the tables they produced.

Compare the tables of each group and see what you can learn from this. Create a table using all the information from the class and calculate the class mean.

 Extension activity: Can pupils, in their groups, think of another activity they could complete to generate data they can use to find out the mean (e.g. jumps in one minute, time to run 50 metres)?

 Recording/evidencing: The tables the pupils create can be stuck into their maths books, along with their working out to answer the questions. Take photographs of the pupils engaged in the activity and store on the school network or in the teacher's online storage system and the pupils' online portfolios. The photographs you took could be annotated to show particular pupils and their progress to understanding mean.

 Assessment methods: Observe the pupils during the activity and record anything of significance. Assess each pupil's ability to create a table, and to use and apply their understanding of mean.

Circles

National Curriculum links

Geometry – properties of shapes

- illustrate and name parts of circles, including radius, diameter and circumference and know that the diameter is twice the radius

- draw shapes accurately, using measuring tools (non-statutory)

Vocabulary	circle, semicircle, circumference, radius, diameter
Resources	selection of string and rope of different thicknesses; builder's pegs; canes; chalk; trundle wheels; metre sticks, 30cm rulers, tape measures; clipboards, centimetre squared paper; compasses; a camera or tablet device per group
Prior learning	understanding of the properties of 2-D shapes
Cross-curricular links	PSHE – cooperation, working as a team, problem solving; Art – collage, looking at pieces of modern art to find circles (e.g. Bridget Riley), creating their own art based on circles, sketching; Science – forces, friction and wheels

Round we go!

Activity

Note: This could be divided into two lessons: finding circles in the environment and creating circles in the environment.

Gather the pupils in the playground and divide them into groups of four. Each group could use a tablet device, and should have a clipboard, pencils and centimetre squared paper. Ask the pupils to elect a group leader who will ensure everyone in the group contributes.

Tell the groups that they will be taking photographs or making sketches and noting the locations of circles and semicircles they see in the playground. Discuss where they might look (e.g. natural objects, wheels on bikes and cars, on play equipment, arches). Give the pupils time to do this.

Look at the photographs or drawings and lists of locations together. Choose one circle and gather so that all the pupils can see it clearly. Feed in the vocabulary of diameter (across the circle and through the middle), radius (centre to the outer rim) and circumference.

Ask the pupils to create a chart to show the radius and diameter of the circles they found. Allow them to choose the most appropriate measuring equipment. Discuss the notion of the semicircle and its relationship to a circle. Be aware of measuring car and bicycle wheels in the school car park – supervise and seek permission from the owner.

Once the activity is complete, ask the pupils about the relationship between the radius and the diameter.

Take the pupils to a grassy area and show them the string, rope, builder's pegs, chalk, canes and measuring equipment. Ask them to use the equipment to make a circle on the grass. They must begin by putting a peg or marker at the centre of the circle. Allow the pupils to experiment, offering support where it is needed. They could mark the circumference with stones, a skipping rope, etc. Try creating circles of a given radius and having another group check the accuracy. Photograph the groups as they take part in the activity.

Bring the pupils together to discuss the challenges and what they have learnt.

 Extension activity: If tablet devices have been used, ask each group to download their photographs of circles into a photo-editing software package or app and label with the measurements. Bring together all the class photographs to create an online class book of circles. Print out the photographs and create a collage. Add photographs of circles inside the school building. Alternatively, ask the pupils to annotate their drawings with the measurements they took and create a class book.

Teach the pupils to use a set of compasses to draw circles with a given radius or diameter.

 Recording/evidencing: The groups will have recorded measurements which can be copied into maths books. Photographs can be printed for maths books. Photographs of the pupils engaged in the activity can be stored in both the pupils' and teacher's online storage system.

 Assessment methods: Observe and talk with the pupils as they work and note anything of significance. Back in the classroom, give each pupil a picture of a blank circle and ask them to label the radius, diameter and circumference.

Number and place value games

National Curriculum links

Number – number and place value

• read, write, order and compare numbers up to 1 000 000 (Year 5) and 10 000 000 (Year 6) and determine the value of each digit

Number – fractions (including decimals and percentages)

• identify the value of each digit in numbers given to three decimal places and multiply and divide numbers by 10, 100 and 1000 giving answers up to three decimal places (Year 6)

Vocabulary	decimal point, digit
Resources	large number of cards (three times the number of pupils) with single digits 0–9 and several additional zeros (underline the digits so that 6 and 9 don't get mixed up); one card with a large dot (the decimal place) on it; a camera or tablet device
Prior learning	some experience of place value and decimals
Cross-curricular links	PSHE – cooperation and working together to solve problems

Let's make a number

Activity

Choose one pupil to be the decimal point. Give the rest of the pupils mixed cards at random and ask them to face the decimal point. (All the games start like this.) Call out a number, and the pupils who have the appropriate cards run to stand either side of the decimal point.

Example (1): Call '736.28'. The five pupils with those digits rush to stand in place. There will be more than one pupil with each digit, so there is competition to get into place quickly before another pupil gets there. This can become very fast and exciting.

Example (2): Call '105.04'. The pupils with the numbered digits run to the appropriate places and the pupils holding zeros take their places in the tens and tenths columns. Not all pupils will quickly see where they are needed. These zeros are the 'place holder zeros', as without them the number is incorrect.

Where are you standing?

Once a number has been made, ask individual pupils to identify where they are standing to see their relationship with the position of the decimal point. They may need to look closely to work out which side of the decimal point they're standing on (e.g. 69270.34). Ask the pupil with the 9, 'Where are you standing?' (They should reply, 'I'm in the thousands place.')

How to multiply and divide by 10, 100, 1000

Call a number and the pupils run into place. Ask the pupils forming the number to multiply or divide by 10 or 100. The decimal place must not move. (This is an important concept and stops pupils thinking they multiply or divide by moving the decimal point.) The rest of the class sees the digits moving to the right or left of the decimal point. Then ask the individuals to identify where they are standing.

Example (1): Call '16.32'. The pupils create the number. Say 'Multiply by 100.' The pupil with the 1 moves to the thousands column and so on. Ask the pupil with the 1, 'Where are you standing?' ('I'm in the thousands place.')

Example (2): Call '240.6'. The pupils create the number. A place holder zero is needed in the ones place. Then say, 'Divide by 10.' The pupils with 2 and 4 move right one place, and the pupil with zero moves to the other side of the decimal point and the pupil with the 6 moves to the hundredths column.

(Place holding zero game supplied by Jeremy D Rowe)

 Extension activity: As understanding and confidence grow, introduce larger numbers and multiplying and dividing by thousands. The class can be divided into ability groups to practise the activities with a pupil as caller.

 Recording/evidencing: Video the activity for later analysis of individual pupil's involvement and store in the teacher's online storage facility as evidence. Ask pupils to record the activity in their maths book and to answer questions (e.g. What happens to the digits when I multiply/divide by 10?).

 Assessment methods: Record observations of pupils during the activity and note anything significant. Analysing any video footage will help you to identify pupils who are secure in these concepts and pupils who need more input.

Acknowledgements

Published by Keen te Books
An imprint of HarperCollins*Publishers Ltd*
The News Building
1 London Bridge Street
London SE1 9GF

ISBN: 9780008238506

First published in 2017

10 9 8 7 6 5 4 3 2 1

Author: Lynn Hannay

The author asserts her moral right to be identified as the author of this work.

Series Concept and Commissioning: Shelley Teasdale and Michelle I'Anson
Project Manager: Fiona Watson
Inside Concept Design: Ian Wrigley
Editor: Susan Milligan
Cover Design: Anthony Godber
Text Design and Layout: QBS Learning
Production: Natalia Rebow

A CIP record of this book is available from the British Library.